## AVAILABLE NOW
## from Lerner Publishing Services!

The *On the Hardwood* series:

Boston Celtics
Brooklyn Nets
Chicago Bulls
Dallas Mavericks
Houston Rockets
Indiana Pacers
Los Angeles Clippers
Los Angeles Lakers

Miami Heat
Minnesota Timberwolves
New York Knicks
Oklahoma City Thunder
Philadelphia 76ers
Portland Trail Blazers
San Antonio Spurs
Utah Jazz

## COMING SOON!

Additional titles in
the *On the Hardwood* series:

Atlanta Hawks
Cleveland Cavaliers
Denver Nuggets
Detroit Pistons
Golden State Warriors
Memphis Grizzlies
Phoenix Suns
Washington Wizards

To Order • www.lernerbooks.com • 800-328-4929 • fax 800-332-1132

# ON THE HARDWOOD

# TRAIL BLAZERS

## J.M. SKOGEN

# On the Hardwood: Portland Trail Blazers

MVP Books
2255 Calle Clara
La Jolla, CA 92037

MVP Books is an imprint of Book Buddy Digital Media, Inc., 42982 Osgood Road, Fremont, CA 94539

MVP Books publications may be purchased for educational, business, or sales promotional use.

Cover and layout design by Jana Ramsay
Copyedited by Susan Sylvia
Photos by Getty Images

ISBN: 978-1-61570-854-3 (Library Binding)
ISBN: 978-1-61570-838-3 (Soft Cover)

# TABLE OF CONTENTS

**B**efore 1970, Portland was not a thrilling place for sports fans. Not only was the NBA completely absent from the great state of Oregon, but there were no major league sports teams at all. Sure, people could look north and root for the Seattle SuperSonics, or they could cheer on the local college teams. But that wasn't the same as having an NBA team of their own.

Then, in February of 1970, everything changed. The NBA was growing, and Portland was on the list of possible cities to receive an expansion team. But Oregon was still considered a very remote place. And the fact that Portland had no other major league sports teams made some NBA owners hesitant to take a chance on the city. Luckily, a born-and-raised Portland sports fan named Harry Glickman decided that it was a risk worth taking.

Harry Glickman was a sports promoter who, in 1960, founded a successful minor league hockey team: the Portland Buckaroos. With so many Portlanders aching for professional basketball, Glickman was certain that they had a great shot at winning a team.

Glickman's dreams of bringing

Harry Glickman (front row, middle) is called the father of professional sports in Portland.

his city into the big leagues took a hit early in 1970, when the NBA upped the cost for an expansion team to $3.7 million. That was nearly double the amount raised by a group of 10 local investors Glickman had assembled. The new figure was far too rich for them.

Desperate, Glickman headed for a meeting with the NBA's expansion committee in Los Angeles, armed only with a shaky,

LaRue Martin was the first overall pick by the Blazers in the 1972 NBA Draft.

alternate financing plan. Weighing heavily on Glickman was a meeting a couple weeks earlier with Seattle businessman, Herman Sarkowsky, a thoroughbred horse breeder. Sarkowsky had indicated he might be interested in backing the team, if two other people he knew would go in with him. He knew a thing or two about taking a gamble. But Glickman hadn't heard from Sarkowsky for several days. He figured it was a longshot, but his only hope.

After the meeting in the Los Angeles hotel room, where questions were raised about the financing plan (and continuing skepticism expressed by some expansion committee members), Glickman left, tired and discouraged. He thought the NBA could very well be passing Portland by again. When he reached the hotel lobby, something happened that changed the history of sports in Portland forever. Harry remembered he had left his raincoat—necessary at home but useless in sunny Los Angeles— in the meeting room. When he went back to retrieve it, one of the owners was on the telephone. "It's for you, Harry. Someone named Sarkowsky is on the line…"

Sarkowsky had great news: the other investors had come through. This was decades before cell phones, so Glickman's lucky timing meant he was there at just the right moment to take the call, and could close the deal with the committee. Glickman later remarked on his good fortune: "So I guess it's fair to say, had I not

Geoff Petrie was one of the best players during the Blazers' early years.

retrieved that raincoat, we might not be in the NBA. I don't know whatever happened to the raincoat, incidentally."

Now that they had a team, Glickman and his investors needed to decide on a name. Two weeks after Portland's expansion team was born, they held a naming

**A Presidential Game**

In 1974, while watching the Trail Blazers beat the Buffalo Braves in Portland, Gerald Ford became the first American president to ever attend an NBA game.

contest. More than 10,000 entries were counted. The top choice was the Pioneers, but it was disqualified because a local college team already had that name. The Trail Blazers, the second-most popular choice at 172 votes, still captured the essence of Oregon's wild and adventurous past. As Portland's only major league team, they were certainly "blazing" a new path in Oregon sports history.

The Blazer's first season was not spectacular, in the sense that they did not immediately post a winning record. But there were many highlights from that first year. They had the best record of the three expansion teams, beating out the Buffalo Braves and the Cleveland Cavaliers. Geoff Petrie, a versatile guard with an exceptional shot, was named co-winner of the 1970-71 NBA Rookie of the Year award. Fans quickly saw that the Blazers were just the kind of spectacle their city had always needed.

Portland had long been known as the Rose City, but during the Blazers' first season, a new name for the city was coined. On February 18, 1971, just about a year after Harry Glickman secured the Blazers for Portland, this young team went up against the L.A. Lakers. The Blazers did not win the game that night. However, in one bold movement during the game, Blazers guard, Jim Barnett, fired up a long baseline jump shot toward the rim. Fans watched the ball arc through the air, sure that it would miss, but willing it to fly through the net. To their amazement, the ball went in. Swish.

Broadcaster Bill Schonely, in that unbelievable moment, cried out "Rip City! All right!" Schonely later said that he didn't even know what "Rip City" was supposed to mean. But one thing was certain—his words, and that fantastic shot, were perfect. Jason Quick, from *The Oregonian*, commented that "Today, Rip City has come to symbolize the connection between Portland and its only major league professional sports team at the time, becoming perhaps as well-known and oft-used as the city's formal moniker, The Rose City." This was just the beginning of Portland's longtime, often frenzied, love for their team.

Then, after an unsuccessful 1973-74 season, Portland received the first pick in the 1974 NBA Draft for their troubles. They used that pick to choose a tall redhead from California. Bill Walton put on the Blazers jersey, and three seasons later he was the leader on a team that changed everything.

Bill Walton's talent and enthusiasm took Portland to a new level.

## Chapter 2
# BLAZERMANIA

June 5th, 1977, was not a normal spring day for the people of Portland, Oregon. They were not outside enjoying the sunshine and 80-degree weather—a treat for those who lived in the often cloudy Pacific Northwest. No, they were inside, gathered around their TVs, watching the Portland Trail Blazers compete in Game 6 of the NBA Finals. Or, if they were lucky, they were one of the 12,888 fans crowded into the sold out Memorial Coliseum. There was even a name for this giddy, nearly hysterical joy that had gripped the town: Blazermania. This was the day their team could become champions.

Led by new head coach, Jack Ramsay, the Blazers had a huge 1976-77 season. This wasn't just

their first visit to the NBA Finals. This was the first time in their seven-year history that Portland had even seen

Dave Twardzik faces off against the Cleveland Cavaliers in a 1977 game.

the postseason. And what a playoff run it had been. After two tightly contested series against the Chicago Bulls and the Denver Nuggets, Portland had torn through the L.A. Lakers in just four games, winning the Western Conference Finals. The Blazers were certainly on fire. They needed to be, for up next were the wildly talented Philadelphia 76ers, led by former ABA star Julius "Dr. J" Erving.

After losing the first two games to the 76ers, the Blazers had managed to climb out of the 0-2 hole and win the next three games. If they won Game 6, they would win it all. The pressure on the players was almost as great as the excitement in the stands. Fans held up signs that said "Red Hot and Rolling" and "Blazermania" and stomped their feet until the arena sounded like the rumbling of a great storm. They were screaming, not just for their team, but for Bill Walton, the "Big Redhead" center who might just carry the Blazers to victory.

Bill Walton had always been thought of as "the next big thing"

Portland Trail Blazers Coach Jack Ramsay signals a play during a 1977 game.

in basketball. Walton was the first and only high-schooler to play on the USA Senior Men's National Basketball Team. He also won the NCAA Player of the Year award three years in a row. So it was no surprise that he was the first draft pick in 1974.

The Portland Trail Blazers knew they had something special with their tall, distinctively redheaded player. However, for the first two years with the Blazers, Walton was constantly injured. It seemed that all of his promise might be wasted. But in 1976-77, Walton was finally and consistently healthy. He showed the NBA just what he could do, leading the Blazers as they cut through the competition, all the way to the NBA Finals.

Bill Walton wore #32 for UCLA, before immortalizing that number in Portland.

Portland needed to get past Julius "Dr. J" Erving to win the 1977 NBA Finals.

created to bring basketball to parts of the country that didn't have an NBA team. But many of these ABA teams wanted to eventually join the more established NBA. On August 5th, 1976, after much negotiating, four of the ABA teams became NBA teams. The other three ABA teams were dissolved, and a special draft was held to find the teamless, yet talented, players new homes.

This wasn't just a big season for the Blazers, but an historic one for the entire NBA. 1976 was the year that the American Basketball Association (ABA) merged with the National Basketball Association (NBA). The ABA was originally

The Philadelphia 76ers traded for Julius "Dr. J" Erving, who had been the ABA's Most Valuable Player from 1974 to 1976. Not to be outdone, the Blazers had traded away several valuable players to have the second pick in the ABA draft. They came away with Maurice "The Enforcer" Lucas, who would prove to be exactly the new blood that Portland needed to take the court with Walton. Lucas, at 6' 9" and 215 pounds, was one of the strongest players in the NBA. He was aggressive, and helped Walton and the Blazers to dominate during their magical 1976-77 season.

The 76ers were hot on the Blazers' heals for most of Game 6. More than once, the crowd was stunned to see "The Doctor" fly past the Blazers' defense for a tricky layup, leaving the announcers to gush about the "magnificence of Julius Erving." But Bill Walton, and the rest of the Blazers, had plenty of moves to show the opposing team. By

**Yum...?**
Bill Walton threw his shirt to the crowd after the 1977 NBA Finals. Maurice Lucas later said, "If I had caught the shirt, I would have eaten it. Bill's my hero."

halftime, the Blazers were leading by 12 points.

However, the 76ers slowly crept

Maurice "The Enforcer" Lucas snatches the rebound against the 76ers during the 1977 NBA Finals.

back into the game in the second half. With only 16 seconds left in the fourth quarter, they were trailing by just two points. A jump ball would go a long way in determining a winner. If Portland gained possession of the ball, it would be easy to run down the shot clock, cutting the time to mere seconds. A momentary stillness came over the arena as the players, and the fans, realized that the 76ers could still come back and win it, pushing the series to a seventh game.

When the 76ers won the jump, Erving grabbed the ball. Suddenly, a big redhead popped out and extended his huge hand, blocking Erving's lane to the basket. Erving twisted past Walton and fired a three-pointer. The ball hit rim, and Portland fans gasped in relief. But the

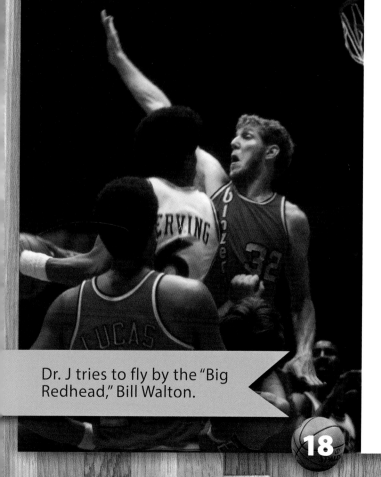

Dr. J tries to fly by the "Big Redhead," Bill Walton.

18

game still wasn't over. The 76ers rebounded, shot, and missed. When the ball went out of bounds, the 76ers had one more chance to tie up the game. With five seconds on the clock, Philadelphia inbounded to McGinnis. But then Maurice "The Enforcer" Lucas stepped up, forming a human wall in front of the basket. McGinnis took the shot, and everyone watched the ball arc through the air…

…and bounce off the rim. It was over. The Blazers were the 1977 NBA Champions!

Even as they announced Portland's victory over the loudspeakers, the fans rushed the court. It looked as though a dam had broken wide open, and the crowd had flooded the hardwood. Bill

Walton actually stripped off his jersey and threw it to the fans. Then he waded, shirtless, through the sea of jumping, screaming, grinning fans, trying to get to the locker room. It must have felt like all of Portland was there, on the court, reaching out their hands— just wanting to be as close to their winning team as possible. And this unbelievable pride for their team has never left. Four decades later, this wild, unstoppable energy is still the trade-mark of Portland's "Blazermaniacs."

# Chapter 3

# BEST IN THE WEST

In May of 1990, Portland was sizzling with Blazermania. Walking down the street, you were sure to hear some news about the Blazers, or a fresh Clyde Drexler statistic. Children drew the Trail Blazers' pinwheel logo in the margins of their school notebooks. Their parents fondly recalled the signs they had made, and the red shirts they had worn to that unforgettable 1977 NBA Championship victory. It had been 13 years since the Blazers—Portland's only professional sports team—were real championship contenders. But now, after racing through the playoffs, Portland would battle the Phoenix Suns to see who would emerge Western Conference Champions.

The Blazers led the series 3-2. However, both of Portland's losses—including one crushing 123-89 defeat—had been in Arizona. When the Blazers headed back to Phoenix

Portland's Terry Porter takes a shot during the 1990 Western Conference Finals.

for Game 6, the city was confident, but a tad nervous. As Portland fans turned on their TVs, or waited by their radios, for some news of the game, one question burned in their minds. Could the Blazers overcome the Suns' home court advantage, and advance to the NBA Finals for the first time since 1977?

When Portland thought back to their first and only championship—and the season that followed—it was with a mixture of pride, sadness, and longing. After capturing the 1977 title, the Blazers had happily embraced their role as defending champions. It was evident they were up to the challenge. By the end of February, the Blazers had won all but 10 of their first 60 games, and were dominating their opponents by an average of 15 points a game. Portland was the talk of the basketball world, and the word "dynasty" was common in most discussions.

However, in the blink of an eye, Portland fans' hopes for a

Bill Walton took home the 1978 MVP award.

championship repeat were dashed. Bill Walton suffered a foot injury and missed the remaining 22 games, as did veteran backup forward Lloyd Neal. Four other starters also sat out numerous games because of injuries. Even though the Trail Blazers won only eight of their remaining 22 games, they still finished with the NBA's best record, 58-24. But they were only a shadow of the team that started the season. Even so, a patched up Blazers lineup kept fans' faint hopes alive—before losing in six games to arch-rival Seattle in the first round of the playoffs.

Bill Walton hobbled through the first two home playoff games before taking a permanent seat on the bench. Those were the last two games he would ever play for the Blazers. After missing the entire 1978-79 season recovering from a stress fracture in his foot, he chose to leave Portland and join the San Diego Clippers. Just

Bill Walton had to sit out the end of the 1977-78 season due to a foot injury.

Bill Walton's #32 jersey was retired by the Portland Trail Blazers in 1990.

like that, the Trail Blazers' MVP was gone, and Portland's status fell from championship contenders to just average. The team still reached the playoffs 25 out of 26 seasons between 1977 to 2004, but before 1990 they usually lost in the first round. Something was missing— some spark that was extinguished when Bill Walton left. The Blazers needed a new star to guide their team.

It would take Portland 13 years to find their way back to the Western Conference Finals. As the players took the court for Game 6 in Phoenix, all eyes were on the Blazers' new leader: Clyde Drexler. Even though the Suns' fans rooted against him, they still appreciated

"Clyde the Glide's" magic on the hardwood.

Clyde Drexler was not always the sure thing that Bill Walton had been. When Drexler first tried out for his freshman basketball team in Houston, Texas, he was only 5' 8". He was not a starter. Instead, he was the 13th man on the team. But by his junior year, after several rapid growth spurts, he was pushing 6' 7", and eventually caught the University of Houston's eye. While at college, Drexler teamed up with future NBA star Hakeem Olajuwon to form "Phi Slama Jama"—a pretend fraternity named for their huge slam dunks and high flying game play. Still, out

Clyde Drexler was famous at the University of Houston for his high flying slam dunks.

of all the NBA teams, only Portland seemed to notice this graceful, talented player from Texas. While Bill Walton was the first pick in the 1974 draft, Clyde Drexler was the

### Living the Dream
When Clyde Drexler played on the 1992 Olympic Dream Team in Barcelona, he added Olympic gold to his list of honors.

14th selection. Drexler later remarked how he kept track of the teams who had overlooked him during the 1983 NBA Draft, and decided to make them regret their decision later on the court.

Coach Jack Ramsay did not often start rookies, so Drexler had limited game time his first year—scoring an unremarkable 7.7 points per game.

Clyde Drexler in his 1984 rookie season.

But he started in 42 games the next season, and by his third year he was an All-Star. By 1988-89, Drexler was scoring 27.7 points per game, and was nicknamed Clyde the Glide for his smooth, effortless attacks on the rim. In 1990, Drexler was more than ready to lead his team to a Western Conference victory.

The Blazers arrived in Phoenix knowing that, if they were going to close the series in six games, they had a huge battle ahead of them. And the Suns' shooting guard, Jeff Hornacek, didn't make their task any easier. Hornacek, in one of the best games of his life, put up 36 points. An announcer exclaimed: "We don't have enough adjectives to describe what Jeff Hornacek has done for this game." With just over one minute left in the fourth quarter, the Suns led 109-106.

Then, as some Phoenix fans began to wonder if they should book plane tickets to Portland for Game 7, the Blazers stepped up. First, Portland's Terry Porter cut the Suns' lead to just one point with a pair of successful free throws. Once Phoenix regained possession of the ball, Hornacek tried to make up those lost points and drove to the rim. However, Clyde Drexler, and teammate Jerome Kersey, had other plans. Kersey stepped up, blocking

Hornacek didn't let the Blazers off easy. He played one of his finest games during the 1990 Western Conference Finals.

Hornacek's shot, then took off across the court. Drexler grabbed the loose ball and fed Kersey, who was ready for the layup. Portland took the lead, 110-109.

### Return to Rip City

In 2010, Buck Williams returned to the Portland Trail Blazers, but in a different capacity. He served as the team's assistant coach for two years.

Portland's Buck Williams was the last player to hold the ball during the 1990 Western Conference Finals.

Portland's Buck Williams grabbed the rebound. As soon as the buzzer sounded, Williams threw the ball into the air, yelling in triumph. The Blazers all rushed the court and dog-piled onto Williams. Even though the Phoenix arena was quiet—saddened by the end of their own season—the Blazers could feel Portland celebrating from 1,000 miles away.

When the Blazers flew home, they found thousands of Blazermaniacs waiting for them at the airport. Scott Lynn, a radio host covering the post-game show, had given Portland a heads up about when the Blazers' plane would land

Portland kept up this momentum, clawing their way to a 112-109 lead. With just six seconds remaining, Phoenix lobbed the ball to their last hope: Jeff Hornacek. He fired a three-pointer—and missed.

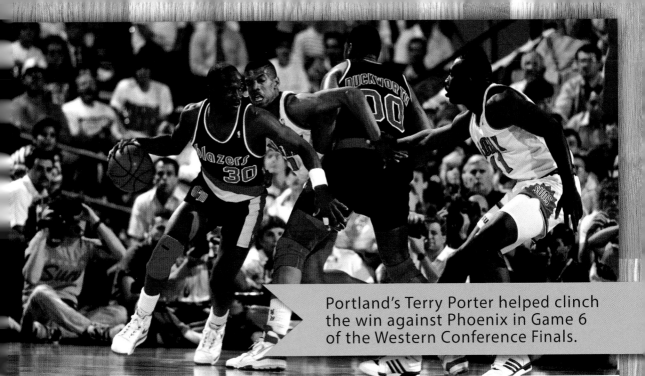

Portland's Terry Porter helped clinch the win against Phoenix in Game 6 of the Western Conference Finals.

at the Hillsboro Airport. Frenzied, and wild with excitement—they even broke a fence after too many people climbed over to reach the tarmac—Blazers fans flocked around their victorious team. Dave Deckard, from the blog, *Blazer's Edge*, recounts how "It took hours to get home that night along the narrow roads winding from the tiny airport but nobody cared. Everyone was delirious. The good guys were about to ascend the mountain again."

Unfortunately, the Blazers were not able to steal the crown from the Detroit Pistons, who were the reigning 1989 champions. But it was clear that this was a new era for the Blazers. They were back on top in the Western Conference—and Portland fans were sure enjoying the view.

# Chapter 4
# CITY OF ROSES

When Paul Allen bought the Portland Trail Blazers in 1988, he was impressed by the dedication and frenzied joy that greeted him at each game. Whether their team was soaring, or on a losing streak, Blazermaniacs came out in huge numbers to show their support. Between 1977 and 1995, Portland sold out every single home game at Memorial Coliseum—adding up to an unbelievable 814 straight games. At the time, this was not only an NBA record, but a record for all American professional sports.

However, Memorial Coliseum was small—holding only 12,888 people—and was not up to current NBA standards. Paul Allen began making plans to build a new arena that could keep up with Rip City's enthusiasm. Allen lived in Seattle, but was famous throughout the entire Pacific Northwest, and the world. Among other accomplishments, he co-founded Microsoft with friend and business partner, Bill Gates. Paul Allen was an exceptional businessman, and had long ago decided to use his billions to make the world a better place. A new arena, Allen hoped, would not only allow more fans to come out and root for the Blazers, but would improve Portland's surrounding district. This area of town is now called the Rose Quarter—a sports and entertainment center that is still developing.

## A Season of Giving

In 2012, Paul Allen was named the most charitable American alive. He gave $372.6 million to charity in 2011!

## The Rose Goes Green

The Rose Garden was the first sports arena to earn the LEED certification (Leadership in Energy and Environmental Design) in 2010.

Paul Allen roots for his team, the Portland Trail Blazers.

Memorial Coliseum had become an important part of the city's cultural history. Originally built in 1960 to honor the veterans of World Wars I and II, it was almost called "The Glass Palace" because of the stunning glass exterior. Some of Rip City's greatest memories—including the 1977 Championship victory, and the 1990 and 1992 trips to the NBA Finals—unfolded between those four walls. So fans were thrilled to learn that, instead of tearing down the old arena, Allen would simply build the new one right next door. Memorial Coliseum is still used by the Portland Winterhawks, a minor league hockey team, and is listed on the National Register of Historic Places. In 2009, the Blazers played a preseason home game at Memorial

Coliseum as part of a 40th anniversary celebration.

Rather than ask Portland to foot the bill for the new arena, Paul Allen paid for most of it himself. To honor Portland's flowery nickname—Rose City— they named the new arena the Rose Garden.

The 1992 NBA Finals were just one of many franchise hightlights that took place in Memorial Coliseum.

During the Rose Garden's Opening Night on November 3rd, 1995, about 20,000 people packed the stands to watch the Blazers take on the Memphis Grizzlies. Fans were given a promotional silver keychain that said "Thank You" and "The Best Fans in Basketball." It wasn't a sudden lack of fan support that ended an almost 20 year sell-out streak—it was because the Rose Garden could hold over 7,000 more people than the Memorial Coliseum.

However, a shiny new arena, and having "The Best Fans in Basketball," didn't mean that the Blazers would instantly hang a second Championship banner. The Blazers'

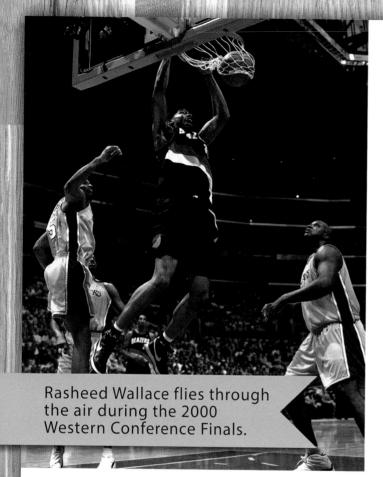

Rasheed Wallace flies through the air during the 2000 Western Conference Finals.

the worst of times to be a Blazers fan during the 2000 Western Conference Finals. The Blazers had a stacked roster—arguably the best team in Blazers history. Power forward Rasheed Wallace, a candidate for Sixth Man of the Year for 1998-99, had stepped up to lead the Blazers in scoring and blocks. Portland had also recently traded for Scottie Pippen—a key player during the Chicago Bulls' three NBA Championships from 1991 to 1993. Pippen had also played with Clyde Drexler and Michael Jordan on the 1992 Olympic Dream Team.

After a rocky start to the series, the Blazers took a firm hold of the reins. Portland overcame a 3-1

records were actually pretty average. The only exceptions were 1999 and 2000, when Portland stormed back to the Western Conference Finals with a power and drive that surprised even their most die-hard fans.

It was the best of times, and

deficit, forcing the Lakers to a decisive seventh game in L.A. If Portland could win Game 7, they would be the first team, ever, to come back from a 3-1 hole to win the Western Conference Finals. With 10:30 left in the fourth quarter, the Blazers were ahead by 15 points. Portland could taste victory. L.A. fans, faced with the cold hard numbers on the scoreboard, began wondering how long it would take to drive home in the post-game traffic.

During the what should have been the Blazers' moment of glory—staging the greatest series comeback in Western Conference Finals history—the Lakers wrote

The Lakers watch helplessly as Scottie Pippen scores with a slam dunk.

their own page in the record books. L.A. stunned the crowds with the largest Game 7 comeback in NBA history. To describe this loss as disappointing would minimize

### Talent by the Dozen
Growing up the youngest of 12 children, Scottie Pippen learned at a young age how to be a part of a team.

the shock and horror felt by every Blazermaniac. Those final 10 and a half minutes—as the Lakers sank everything they threw at the net—were devastating.

After this bitter loss, Scottie Pippen tried to put their season ending game into perspective:

A young Blazers fan roots for Scottie Pippen.

"Nobody expected us to push them so hard. Nobody gave us a chance when we were down 3-1. There's more to feel proud of than there is to be down about." Sure, this was a day in Blazers history that many fans would like to forget. But that would mean discounting what a fantastic team the Blazers had assembled.

After such a spirit-crushing start to the new millennium, the Blazers' staff decided to shake up the roster—trying to find an instant fix that would finally lead them back to the NBA Finals. What followed were some of the worst years that the Blazers have ever seen. After several more first-round playoff exits—with turmoil on and off the court—they started missing the postseason altogether in 2004. The Blazers' 2004 absence ended a 20-year playoff streak, and they would not climb their way back into the playoffs until 2009.

When Portland ended the 2005-06 season with an NBA-worst 21-61 record, it was clear that the Blazers required a new strategy. They needed young players who could work together toward a great future. Wayne Thompson's book, *Blazermania*, describes the Blazers' amazing 2006 NBA Draft Day: "In perhaps the most active and successful day of deal-making in league history, Steve

Patterson and [Kevin] Pritchard executed six deals involving six teams, 13 players, and five draft choices, literally building a future playoff contender in a matter of 24 hours."

LaMarcus Aldridge and Brandon Roy sign autographs, shortly after being chosen by the Blazers in the 2006 NBA Draft.

# Chapter 5
## FRANCHISE ON THE RISE

At the end of that franchise-changing 2006 NBA Draft Day, Portland had acquired two players who became the face of the Portland Trail Blazers: Brandon Roy and LaMarcus Aldridge. Like Bill Walton, Brandon Roy was always a star. Roy's family raised him to value sports and athleticism, and he quickly became a leader on his Seattle high school basketball team. After scoring 38 points in the final game of his senior year, Roy was forced to choose between immediately entering the NBA Draft, or attending college. He ultimately decided to stay close to home, and give

his game time to improve. Roy put on the University of Washington's purple and gold jersey, and Seattle rejoiced.

In 2006, after ending his college days as Pac-10 Player of the Year, Roy became the sixth pick in the NBA Draft. When Minnesota

Before Brandon Roy was a star in Portland, he made a name for himself as a Husky in Seattle.

The Blazers did not return to the playoffs immediately after the 2006 NBA Draft, but it was clear that they were on the right track. Brandon Roy was a sensation—claiming the NBA's 2006-07 Rookie of the Year after re-ceiving 127 of 128 first place votes. Roy continued to rack up honors, appearing in three All-Star games between 2008 and 2010. He also won the hearts of the Blazermaniacs with his fearless shooting and confident smile.

Greg Oden, Portland's #1 pick in the 2007 NBA Draft, was an instant hit with the Blazermaniacs.

swapped Roy to Portland as part of a complicated draft day trade, the Timberwolves couldn't have known what kind of talent they had just given away.

In 2007, Portland used their #1 draft pick to further stack their roster with seven-foot tall, 285-pound Greg Oden. This huge center was supposed to be the third pillar of Portland's rebuilding franchise. A billboard near the Rose Garden proclaimed "The Road Back to Rip City," with huge pictures of Oden, Roy, and Aldridge. By 2009, the Blazers were playoff contenders once again.

Unfortunately, Brandon Roy proved to have even more in common with NBA great Bill Walton, and was plagued with injuries throughout his NBA career. Before the start of the 2011-12 season, Roy discovered that his knees were so badly damaged that he would require several surgeries. There was a very real chance that he would never be able to play

## Honk Once

Before the 2007 NBA Draft, a Portland billboard asked drivers to honk once for Greg Oden, and twice for Kevin Durant. Portland chose Oden, and Seattle used their second draft pick to snag Durant.

Brandon Roy celebrates after a victory in the 2011 NBA playoffs.

basketball again. In a heartbreaking decision, Roy chose to focus on his health, and announced his retirement from the NBA. Portland mourned the loss of their star shooting guard, but wished him a safe recovery with his wife and two young children.

Devastating health issues also struck Portland's other great hope: Greg Oden. Before the 2007-08 season even started, Oden suffered season-ending knee damage. Though he would recover in time for the 2008-09 season, this was the start of a pattern of injury that ultimately ended Oden's career with the Blazers. During his five seasons on Portland's roster, Oden only played a total of 82 games—the equivalent of one regular season. When he was healthy, Oden played

When Greg Oden was healthy, he played with a power that was almost unmatched in the NBA.

with the kind of dominating talent that made fans wistful about what might have been. Finally, after many injuries and setbacks, Portland was forced to waive Oden in 2012 to clear space for new talent on the roster. Of the three building blocks on their "Road Back to Rip City," only LaMarcus Aldridge remained.

While Brandon Roy and Greg Oden often took the spotlight, LaMarcus Aldridge was also a vital part of the team. Though many Blazermaniacs' first introduction to Aldridge was during that groundbreaking 2006 NBA Draft, Aldridge's path to the NBA began years earlier, as an eighth grader in

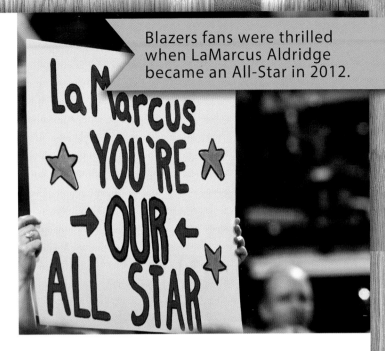

Blazers fans were thrilled when LaMarcus Aldridge became an All-Star in 2012.

Texas. A coach took an interest in LaMarcus, and convinced his mother to send him to Seagoville—a high school with a great sports program. During his freshman year, Aldridge worked hard to earn a starting position, and ultimately walked

### On the Mend

When Roy retired, Portland used an amnesty clause to release him from their roster. His knees later improved, but he couldn't return to the Blazers. Instead, he joined the team that originally drafted him: Minnesota.

away with his team's MVP award. He arrived at practice early, and often hit the gym again in the evenings after getting off work at a shoe store. *Sports Illustrated's* Chris Mannix reported how, one night, during a power outage at the gym, "Aldridge opened the doors so that there was enough moonlight to see the rim."

LaMarcus Aldridge, or L.A., as his fans called him, brought that same level of determination to Portland, and constantly worked to raise the level of his game. Between his first and second seasons, Aldridge's points per game leaped from nine to 17.8—nearly snagging him the Most Improved Player of the Year award. Before the 2010-11 season, after assessing his own weaknesses on the court, Aldridge put in some hard hours with a trainer who usually worked with football players. That year, after bulking up with six extra pounds of muscle, Aldridge averaged 21.8

LaMarcus Aldridge: the new leader of the Portland Trail Blazers.

The Blazers' mascot, Blaze the Trail Cat, kicks off the 2012-13 season in style.

points per game. With Roy retired, and Greg Oden sidelined, it was Aldridge who stepped up and took the helm. Though the Blazers went through a rough transition without Roy in the 2011-12 season—missing the playoffs for the first time since 2008—LaMarcus continued to grow as a player. In 2012, Aldridge was elected to the Western Conference All-Star team.

After that disappointing 2011-12 season, Portland searched for new players who could provide the much needed support for Aldridge on the hardwood. In a move that reminded many fans of the 2006 NBA Draft Day juggling act, the Blazers replaced over half of their roster before the

### Scared Stiff!
Ever since a visit to a wax museum, Damian Lillard has been afraid of statues of historic figures.

Damian Lillard helps the Blazers crush the Lakers during their 2012-13 season opener on Halloween.

Lillard's goal had always been to play in the NBA, he did not take the easiest path. For a short time, Lillard went to the same private high school that NBA great, Jason Kidd once attended. When the coach did not give Lillard enough playing time, Lillard made the decision to transfer to a public school. He didn't want his talents to rot from always sitting on the bench. At Oakland High School, things got better. Lillard started playing, and playing well. He then earned a scholarship to Weber State—a small college in Ogden, Utah. Four years later, Lillard became the 15th NBA player to emerge from Weber State, and the first ever to be selected in

2012-13 season. Only seven players remained from the previous year. LaMarcus Aldridge summed up the 2012-13 Blazers team: "New pieces, new players…new coach. Everything's new."

One of these "new talents" was rookie Damian Lillard—the sixth pick in the 2012 draft. Though

the first round of the NBA Draft.

There was a lot of hype surrounding Lillard's arrival, and he tried to live up to fans' expectations. He played like a phenom right away, becoming the third rookie to ever tally more than 20 points and 10 assists in his first NBA game. After this first stunning game, Lillard more than lived up to expectations all season. As proof, he took home the 2012-13 NBA Rookie of the Year award.

With this exciting new roster, Blazermaniacs have bright hopes for the future. If Portland continues to cultivate young, talented players like Damian Lillard, and if veterans like

LaMarcus Aldrige can stay injury-free, then the Blazers could rejoin the ranks of the NBA's greatest. After a 43-year journey of high peaks and low valleys, the Portland Trail Blazers' second championship might be just around the bend.

Damian Lillard and LaMarcus Aldridge: the future of the Portland Trail Blazers.